Stressed to the Max

Peace for Women under Pressure

Joni Eareckson Tada

New
Growth
Press

www.newgrowthpress.com

New Growth Press, Greensboro, NC 27404
www.newgrowthpress.com
Copyright © 2013 by Joni Eareckson Tada

All Scripture quotations, unless otherwise indicated, are taken from the *Holy Bible,* New International Version®, NIV®. Copyright © 1973, 1978, 1984, 2011 by Biblica, Inc. Used by permission. All rights reserved worldwide.

Scripture quotations marked KJV are taken from the King James Version of the Bible.

Cover Design: Faceout books, faceout.com
Typesetting: Lisa Parnell, lparnell.com

ISBN-10: 1-939946-09-3
ISBN-13: 978-1-939946-09-6

Library of Congress Cataloging-in-Publication Data
Tada, Joni Eareckson.
  Stressed to the max : peace for women under pressure / author
Joni Eareckson Tada.
      pages cm
  Includes bibliographical references and index.
  ISBN 978-1-939946-09-6 (alk. paper)
  1. Christian women—Religious life. 2. Stress management for
women. 3. Stress management—Religious aspects—Christianity.
I. Title.
  BV4527.T325 2013
  248.8'6—dc23   2013018370

Printed in South Korea

25 24 23 22 21 20 19   5 6 7 8 9

December was upon us and my husband Ken had been planning our vacation to Hawaii for months. He had shown me every possible brochure of "things to do" on Maui, including a drive to the top of the Haleakala Crater to see a 5:00 a.m. sunrise. He had checked and double-checked our reservations at the Sheraton-Maui and had called Wheelchair Getaways five times to confirm our van rental. He was even "gifting" me with a friend to go along to help with my needs. My husband was *excited.* "Joni, I want to do everything I can to make sure *you* have a good time!"

Now the long-awaited day of departure had arrived. With me in my wheelchair tied in the back of our van, my friend sitting nearby, and suitcases piled all around, Ken drove us down the 101 Freeway to LAX airport. Since it was early afternoon and I knew the Joni and Friends office was open, I was asking my friend to help me check my iPhone for emails all the way to the 405 interchange.

"What are you doing back there?" Ken said to me in the rearview mirror. His voice had a slight edge. "You're not working, are you?" Our eyes met in the mirror, and I sheepishly put away my phone. After a long minute he sighed, "Joni, you've been so busy; it's important that you take a break. You *need* this break."

What I need is to have my computer on this trip, I inwardly groused. And so as we were speeding down the 405 Freeway and Ken and my friend jabbered about the fun things we would do, I kept wondering how I would find time to keep up with emails, rearrange deadlines, write a new message for a holiday speaking engagement, and—oh yes—shop for Christmas. *How am I going to do* that *in Hawaii?!* I felt my throat tighten with the pressure. *I do not have time for this. A vacation isn't alleviating anything; it's only adding more stress.*

When we got off the plane in Maui, the Wheelchair Getaways van we ordered was late in arriving. We had to sit curbside for a good half hour. So while my husband made a call to the van rental place, I snuck out my iPhone to check on things at the office. One or two emails required an immediate response, so I hacked out quick replies.

Minutes later we were loaded up and driving along the coast to our hotel. I was struck by the aquamarine color of the sea and the huge clouds above the smaller island of Lanai in the distance. Still I kept thinking, *This vacation is just plain inconvenient. Timing couldn't be worse.*

The next morning I slept in. I was stunned at how late I slept, but the bed was comfortable and the sheets were nice and soft. After a leisurely brunch, we strolled the walkway along the beach. I put my wheelchair on slow speed, stopped often at the tourist kiosks, inhaled the sea air, and listened to the clicking of palm fronds above us. As we walked on, I asked to see my iPhone, but it was dead. *No problem; I'll do it later.*

But later came and went, and I never got around to plugging it in.

For the rest of the week Ken and I lingered by the pool and sipped smoothies. He talked me into snorkeling (frightening for a quadriplegic like me). When he flipped me facedown in the water, I spotted a giant sea turtle just ten feet away! Five minutes earlier or later and I would've missed him. *Thank you, Lord! You are so good to me!* I got in the pool, visited the spa, and ordered more smoothies. I didn't check my emails once.

I came home revived and inspired by a vacation that I was too stressed to even know that I needed. We can't all just take off for Hawaii whenever we are stressed—much as I wish we could—but that experience taught me what I was missing in my daily life and made me eager to get back to living the way God wants me to live. To be able to say, *Thank you, Lord! You are so good to me!* in the middle of my everyday life. Is it possible to learn to live like this when you are not on vacation? In the Bible, God says yes. And he promises us that as we ask him for help, he will give it freely.

Are You Stressed?

Perhaps you, like me, are tired and stressed and don't even realize it. Or maybe you do, but you keep plowing ahead anyway, living on yesterday's energy. You have plenty of company. Women today are more stressed than ever before. We wonder why we still look exhausted after a solid night's sleep. When we do try to slow down, life seems to overtake us, and we find ourselves scrambling to keep up. No wonder we feel worn out before lunchtime.

Part of it is that we are under more pressure than we were even twenty years ago. Modern life back in the '90s included time-saving appliances such as microwaves, fax, and answering machines. These things were convenient and designed to give us more time off. But, in fact, these gadgets only *speeded up* life. Nowadays, iPads, voice messaging, texting, and smartphones with email capabilities have *increased* the speed of life.

Technology should—and in many ways does—make our lives better. We organize our work and personal appointments on our computer, we pay our bills electronically, and we keep up with our friends through Facebook. But while we are streaming content from the Internet as the robotic vacuum sucks dog hair from under the couch, we end up crowding the extra hours afforded by these conveniences with more commitments. We have more time to *do* more. There is exercising at Zumba class, baking for the church sale, watching our kids' soccer-baseball-basketball practices, singing at choir rehearsals, and—the biggie—working additional hours.

People's expectations of us are higher too. After all, we are in touch with many more individuals who, because we've "friended" them on Facebook, expect a real relationship. Our inbox is clogged with emails from people we hardly know, yet are asking for an immediate reply.

The pressures of working, maintaining marriage responsibilities, parenting, keeping our appearance, running a modern household, and nurturing friendships all seem more intense. So if you feel weary, you're not alone. Welcome to the modern world.

What Is Stress?

Stress is an unavoidable part of life. It has helped humans survive for thousands of years, and it keeps us on our toes in dangerous or critical situations. Consider the following basics:

- In response to stressful stimuli, your body turns on its biological response. Chemicals and hormones are released that help your body rise to the challenge. Your heart rate increases, your brain works faster and becomes razor sharp, and you have a sudden burst of energy. This response is natural and basic (it's what kept our ancestors from falling victim to hungry predators).
- Stress is subjective; something that may be stressful for one person—like speaking in public—may not be stressful for someone else.
- Stress overload, however, can have harmful effects. Too much stress can cause potentially serious physical and mental health problems.

It is a good thing when you respond to a true danger—like a car coming out of nowhere to broadside you—with increased heart rate and a sudden burst of energy. God made you to respond quickly in a crisis. But we are not meant to live as if we are in constant danger. The good news is that stress *can* be avoided and is usually manageable if you are able to recognize and take control of pressure-riddled situations. The goal isn't to get rid of stress completely. That would be impossible. Instead, stress management may be as simple—yet as powerful—as changing your focus. Let's take a look.

Are You Spiritually Worn Out?

Our electronic world often influences the way we relate to God. We "abide in him" as though we were charging our smartphone or our iPad. We think, *How long do I have to be plugged into God today through a quiet time or prayer in order to get enough of a spiritual charge?* But Jesus doesn't say "I am the power cord and you are the cell phone." He says, "I am the vine; you are the branches" (John 15:5).

Life in Christ is not a matter of going to a conference to "get our spiritual batteries charged." We don't go to Bible study so we can live off its spiritual energy for a week until we require another surge of divine power. That's not the metaphor the Bible invites us to use. We are branches that are *connected* to Christ, the Vine. And with him, there can never be any disconnect. Abiding is living in constant awareness of total dependence. Abiding is all about a relationship. But how do we abide? Looking at the familiar story of Martha and Mary in the Bible can help us understand how to change our focus to abiding with Christ, rather than all the things we have to get done.

Frazzled, Tired, and Cranky

When I read those three words, I think of Martha in the Bible. As Mary's older sister she was the chief cook and bottle washer in a home where there was no parent to clean up after anyone. She was one busy woman! Once, when Jesus and his disciples were visiting, Martha pulled out all the stops to entertain them. But where was her sous chef-sister? Mary had left the kitchen and snuck into the living room to hear Jesus.

That's when Martha lost it. Luke 10:40–41 records that "She came to [Jesus] and asked, 'Lord, don't you care that my sister has left me to do the work by myself? Tell her to help me!'" It's almost a comical picture: Mary with hands on hips, stomping into the living room and demanding that her honored guest drop everything to help her sort out problems in the kitchen. This was one frazzled, tired, and cranky woman.

But I'm going to stick up for Martha. I believe she was on the right path, even with her *much* serving, as the Bible puts it. We can never do enough in God's kingdom, and Martha is not to be chided for rolling up her sleeves to prepare a meal for such an honored guest as the Lord Jesus.

The problem was her focus. Luke 10:40 says, "But Martha was distracted by all the preparations that had to be made." Did you get that? She "was *distracted* by all the preparations." It wasn't that she was too busy or planned too many things on the menu. Hustle and bustle wasn't the culprit. Martha simply allowed those things to distract her from focusing on the Savior. She lost joy in her labor, gladness in ministering to her Lord, and delight in exercising her gift for the good of the group. A complaining spirit took over as she focused on her sister Mary, along with all the pots and pans!

It requires spiritual discipline and an adoration for the Savior *not* to become encumbered by hounding pressures and demands. But it can be done. Great Christians of the past—and many in the present—have worn their fingers to the bone in the advancement of Christ's kingdom while maintaining a tranquil spirit and an unyielding focus on Christ. It is possible to be busy—even *very* busy—and not let stress make you tired, frazzled, and cranky. How is that possible? To illustrate, let me tell you another story.

Life . . . One Day at a Time

My friend Becky was injured in an automobile accident some time ago. I remember when she was going through all the painful adjustments to life in a wheelchair. She'd hoped to go to graduate school once she became acclimated to her wheelchair. She was loaded with beauty and brains, but that didn't make coping with her new and challenging situation any easier. One day she let down her guard with me and spilled out some of the frustration.

"Joni, how will I ever keep up with the pace of my classes when I go to graduate school? And it's downright tiring always having to ask for help. I'm not sleeping at night, I've got a pressure sore that's on my backside, and . . . and my slacks don't fit!"

Becky had to learn what I learned after my accident: take life one day at a time. I told her, "Don't try to live your life all at once. You can't resolve graduate school, finances, insomnia, and paralysis-problems all in one day. Take life in bite-size chunks that you can swallow. And *trust* that the Lord is in the details."

Many of us want life to go as smoothly as cruising down a freeway with nary a pothole or stoplight in sight. But life's not like that. Life is usually one detour after the next that forces you onto exits you never planned for and into territory without a road map.

Becky is dealing with *a lot* of stress in her life, and in a way, she's being forced to learn the art of letting go. She is learning to release her ambitions, orderly plans, some relationships, and, for now, hopes of graduate school. Yes, she may get there, but God has more important things for her to deal with—like living one day at a time on this new detour. As a Puritan pastor once wrote, "Contentment is the ability to appreciate the scenery on life's detours."[1]

It's the way God *intends* for us to live. Lamentations 3:22–24 says, "Because of the LORD's great love we are not consumed, for his compassions never fail. They are new every morning; great is your faithfulness. I say to myself, 'The LORD is my portion; therefore I will wait for him.'" There is no grace available for next year's problems or next month's challenges or tomorrow's demands. *There is only grace for today.* God gives fresh energy moment-by-moment, starting as soon as you throw back the covers in the morning. Let's unpack Lamentations 3:22–24 a bit more.

- If you allowed the pressures around you to rule the day, or took on more than you could possibly

handle, you would be *consumed.* But because of
the Lord's great love, you are promised *strength
for the day.* Remember Deuteronomy 33:25, "as
thy days, so shall thy strength be" (kjv). Start
by thanking God at the end of each day for the
strength he gave you.

- His compassions *never fail.* The Lord may have put
Becky (and you!) on a new and frightening detour,
but it's still his Plan A for you both. God always
has our best in mind. His promises never fail, and
God will be with Becky through every twist and
turn. What are the roadblocks that are forcing you
onto an inconvenient detour? Be encouraged, for
the road signs read *It's All in God's Plan!*

- The Lord is your portion for *today.* God's purpose
for you is that you depend on him and his power
now. Remember that he is the vine and you are
the branch. God may not be necessarily working toward a particular finish weeks or months
ahead; rather, his end is *the process.* God's training
is for *now,* not tomorrow. His purpose is for this
minute, not always something in the future. Such
a perspective helps you live life one day at a time.
What is looming on your horizon that causes
anxiety or fear? Remember, God has not given
you grace to handle that future challenge—only
grace for today.

How is Becky doing now? Well, she never made it to
graduate school, but she ended up meeting a wonderful
guy while in rehab. He's a physical therapist who fell in

love with this charming, gutsy, good-looking girl who wheeled into his PT lab. They now attend church in Southern California and are actively involved in reaching out to other couples who are facing catastrophic injuries and illnesses in their marriage. Way to go, Becky. Your detour never was God's Plan B. It was his best plan all the time. And you got there, unfrazzled, taking one day at a time.

Stress Decompression: Waiting on the Lord

I am so grateful to God for my paralysis because in many ways, it regulates areas of pressure in my life. To be sure, quadriplegia can *add* a great many responsibilities and challenges—which can mean more stress— but for the most part, my wheelchair *forces* me to slow down.

I wait in bed for my friend to come and help me get up in the morning . . . I wait for medical appointments . . . I wait for others to empty my leg bag, help me with lunch, set my work in front of me, and give me sips of coffee. At the close of the day, I wait for my husband to help me lay down at night. This can't help but impose a slower pace to my days. My disability requires me to live according to Galatians 5:25, "Since we live by the Spirit, let us keep in step with the Spirit." To keep in step with the Holy Spirit is to obey the pace *he* sets for the day. And *that* definitely dissipates stress. To keep in step with the Spirit requires you to:

- *Invite God to rule your day.* Listen to his promptings, not only first thing in the morning but throughout the day. Remember, live life in small, swallow-able chunks.

- *Abide in Jesus as a branch abides in a vine.* Stay connected by asking God questions throughout the day such as, "Lord, should I say no to this request?" or "What are your priorities for my afternoon?" Each hour of the day will present different demands, so make it a habit to ask for his guidance in not only great, but small matters.
- *Be sensitive to warnings from your conscience,* especially when you find yourself in volatile situations. For instance, you may decide to back away from an argument, knowing it will only lead to more tension. Diffuse anger as soon as possible.
- *Realize God is mostly interested in your relationship with him and others.* Yes, he's concerned about your job performance, home responsibilities, and church commitments. But the core of his concern is the way you *relate* to him and others throughout your day.

Waiting on the Lord is like releasing the valve on a pressure cooker. But waiting on the Lord goes *so* against our human grain. You may want to impulsively add something to your already crowded schedule. But the truth is that you really don't want to check in with the Lord, discern his mind and his desires, and wait for his green light.

Ah, but while we may regret a hasty decision a million times over, we will never regret waiting on the Lord. You can never go wrong as you wait and pray and still yourself in his presence, seeking his mind and heart. He'll end up giving you something better. He will give you wisdom as well as himself. And when you have apprehended him in a new, fresh way, it will all come clear. The choice will be obvious. The waiting will be worth it.

What you might provide for yourself by your effort, in your wisdom and in your timing, cannot be compared to what God has for you in his plan and his timing. Are you at a crossroads of decision in your life? Are you dealing with a need that's pushing you to hurry or add something more to your schedule? Fight the temptation to run ahead of him. Lay your desires and petitions at his feet and wait for his peace (Philippians 4:6–7).

A Biblical Way to Manage Stress

When we wait on the Lord, we're waiting on his *wisdom*. Proverbs 8:34 says, "Blessed is the man who listens to me [Wisdom], watching daily at my doors, waiting at my doorway." When a new morning dawns, watch daily at God's door, for he has your day's agenda. And he knows best how to order your hours.

After all, God created us and he understands our body's stress mechanisms inside and out. He's the one who gave us the "flight or fight" reaction in the first place. Thankfully, God wrote the book on stress management, and the Bible is filled with wise counsel on how to deal with anxiety, tension, pressure, and fear. Consider these steps:

1. *Ask the Holy Spirit to reveal if you are under chronic stress.* "Search me, O God, and know my heart; test me and know my anxious thoughts. See if there is any offensive way in me, and lead me in the way everlasting" (Psalm 139:23–24).

2. *Pinpoint areas in your life that are creating tension, weariness, and anxiety.* "Be still, and know that I am God; I will be exalted among the nations, I will be exalted in the earth" (Psalm 46:10).

3. *Ask the Spirit to show you how you can better manage those stressful areas.* "Teach us to number our days, that we may gain a heart of wisdom" (Psalm 90:12).

4. *Read the Bible with an eye on those passages and scriptural examples of Spirit-inspired stress management.* "Trust in the LORD with all your heart and lean not on your own understanding; in all your ways submit to him, and he will make your paths straight" (Proverbs 3:5–6).

5. *Take prayerful, significant steps to help you avoid stress.* "Do not be anxious about anything, but in every situation, by prayer and petition, with thanksgiving, present your requests to God" (Philippians 4:6).

Just Do What You Can

Sometimes after a busy day, I lie on my pillow and wonder, *Am I doing this thing called "the Christian life" right? Am I living as I should? Doing what I should be doing?*

I found a reassuring answer in Mark chapter 14. It was an event that occurred before Christ's crucifixion. Jesus was visiting the home of Simon the Leper when a woman entered and poured expensive perfume on Jesus' head. Those gathered there were indignant over such a waste of good perfume (this wasn't cheap toilet water; this was the real thing). "'Leave her alone,' said Jesus. 'Why are you bothering her? She has done a beautiful thing to me. . . . She did what she could. She poured perfume on my body beforehand to prepare for my burial. Truly I tell you, wherever the gospel is preached throughout the world, what she has done will also be told, in memory of her'" (Mark 14:6–9).

The people in that room thought the woman had done a stupid thing. I identify with her. Often I feel as though I have done stupid things in my service to the Lord. *Am I doing this right? Does this really count? Am I doing it in the right spirit?* But like the woman in Mark chapter 14, I have done what I could. That's all God asks. We can only do what we are *able* to do. But when it's work offered with an eye to God's glory, it's always a beautiful thing in Jesus' sight.

Sometimes we feel guilty if we can't accomplish everything that we hope to for the Lord. And so we keep adding more things to our schedule. So if you are feeling weary and tired of trying, *do what you can* in service to Christ. It will be enough.

Tips for Finding Fresh Energy

It is often easier to say "do what you can" than it is to figure out what that should look like. Here are some practical things to do when you feel stressed that can turn your heart and mind toward Christ, as well as minimize stressors in your life.

- *Prayer and Meditation* – "I meditate on your precepts and consider your ways" (Psalm 119:15). This is possible even with a packed schedule. Give yourself some silent time to talk to God and let your thoughts dwell on him and his Word, even focus on your breathing. This small amount of peace can help you deal with or release stress. Think of three things that the Lord has done for you, meditate on each thing for at least a minute, and praise God for each blessing.

- *Organize your Life* – "Let all things be done decently and in order" (1 Corinthians 14:40 KJV). Get rid of the clutter, one room at a time. Make lists and stick to them. Get a daily planner so you can keep tabs on your appointments. I find that it helps to frequently refer to your "month at a glance" page so that you'll be able to schedule in blocks of free time.

- *Eat Healthy* – "Daniel then said to the guard . . . 'Please test your servants for ten days: Give us nothing but vegetables to eat and water to drink. Then compare our appearance with that of the young men who eat the royal food, and treat your servants in accordance with what you see'" (Daniel 1:11–13). It's been proven that junk food can make us depressed (not to mention fat), so clean up your diet. Healthy foods like whole grains and protein can improve your mood and give you long-lasting energy to tackle everything that comes your way during the day.

- *Exercise* – "She sets about her work vigorously; her arms are strong for her tasks" (Proverbs 31:17). Exercise gives you the time to be alone with your thoughts (or an opportunity to let them go). Physical training also has the added benefit of releasing endorphins into the brain, which improves your mood.
- *Sleep* – "I lie down and sleep; I wake again, because the LORD sustains me" (Psalm 3:5). This may be the most important natural stress reducer of them all. Too little sleep leaves us cranky, irritable, and on edge. Too much sleep can leave us sluggish and depressed. Find the right balance that allows you to feel well-rested and ready for the day.
- *Music* – "It is good to praise the LORD and make music to your name, O Most High" (Psalm 92:1). Your favorite tunes can be an enjoyable, passive route to stress relief. Creating playlists for various moods (a cathartic mix for when you want to process feelings, an upbeat mix for when you need more energy, etc.) can help you to relieve stress passively, enjoyably, and conveniently. Put on some praise music and spend time praising the Lord.

Dry Times

Every woman I know has experienced dry times. During these times the Bible seems as inspiring as the Los Angeles phone book and prayer feels like an exercise in futility. I had one of those dry times not long ago, and it seemed as though my prayers couldn't even reach the ceiling, let alone heaven.

I listened to my Christian friends talk about how they were learning and growing and what God was telling them and *wasn't the Lord wonderful?* I tried to listen hard, but faking it made me feel even more guilty.

The hardest part was that I could not trace the dry spell to anything specific. No besetting sin that had entangled me. No fights with my husband. No root of bitterness over my disability. No great lapses in my prayer life or Bible study. And certainly not a lack of fellowship. Yet my spirit felt as arid as July in the desert. Maybe you can identify. Your smile loses its shine, your soul becomes dim, and your countenance tells you and everyone around you that something's not quite right.

Strange as it sounds, the closest biblical analogy I can find for those dry days takes place in the middle of a lake. Let's pick up the story in Luke 5.

> [Jesus] got into one of the boats, the one belonging to Simon, and asked him to put out a little from shore. Then he sat down and taught the people from the boat. When he had finished speaking, he said to Simon, "Put out into deep water, and let down the nets for a catch." Simon

answered, "Master, we've worked hard all night and haven't caught anything. But because you say so, I will let down the nets." When they had done so, they caught such a large number of fish that their nets began to break. So they signaled their partners in the other boat to come and help them, and they came and filled both boats so full that they began to sink. When Simon Peter saw this, he fell at Jesus' knees and said, "Go away from me, Lord; I am a sinful man!" (5:3–8)

That's a story for dry times. It's a story for when you feel tired of trying, when you're weary of praying prayers that don't seem to get answered, when the pages of the Bible might as well be written in hieroglyphics.

Simon was weary. He was tired of trying. His back ached and his eyelids drooped. Yes, he had heard the Master preach to the people just moments before, but still he lacked faith and confidence in Jesus' words. Besides, he had been up all night without so much as a sardine to show for it. Yet at the command of Christ he was able to summon what little energy he had left and let down his net one more time.

As a wife, mother—or as a single woman working downtown—perhaps your net is empty today. You've been trying to resolve a conflict at home, catch up with the dishes and laundry, finish the week's errands, but there just don't seem to be enough hours in the day. You feel dry and deflated, and you wonder if God has misplaced your file somewhere on his desk.

He hasn't! God has been actively engaged moment-by-moment every step of the way. He has been working behind the scenes, shifting hearts and pushing souls and prodding unwilling spirits. He has been laboring specifically and intentionally with a clear goal in mind for your life, as well as the life of your family and your neighbors and your coworkers. Just be encouraged; those petitions you offered during the dry times have pleased him best.

Your heavy heart is no secret to the God who loves you. As David wrote, "All my longings lie open before you, oh Lord; my sighing is not hidden from you" (Psalm 38:9).

He is asking you today to let down your net. One more time. Even though you haven't seen amazing results in recent weeks. Even though your emotions say, *What's the use?* Even though running an uphill marathon seems more appealing than seeking the Lord right now. Nevertheless, *obey* the word of Christ and let down your net. Keep in the Word. Hit your knees and return to prayer. Confess your sins of unbelief (not to mention a sour, skeptical attitude). Get into a closer relationship of accountability with a trusted Christian friend. Do some little, special thing for your husband and children. Worship your God this coming Sunday morning with a hands-down, slam-dunk amazement over his grace to you and every other sinner in your congregation.

Sooner or later, he'll surprise you just as he surprised Simon Peter. He's going to bring you out of that long night—out of that dryness. You're going to experience his joy—more joy than you can handle. So be faithful, friend. Trust him. Wait on him.

Jesus can still fill an empty net. And when he does, don't forget to say, *Thank you, Lord. You are so good to me!*

Endnotes

1. Edythe Draper, *Draper's Book of Quotations for the Christian World* (Wheaton, IL: Tyndale House Publishers, 1992), 101. George Herbert is the name of the pastor quoted.

Simple, Quick, Biblical

Advice on Complicated Counseling Issues for Pastors, Counselors, and Individuals

MINIBOOK
CATEGORIES

- Personal Change
- Marriage & Parenting
- Medical & Psychiatric Issues

- Women's Issues
- Singles
- Military

USE YOURSELF | GIVE TO A FRIEND | DISPLAY IN YOUR CHURCH OR MINISTRY

New Growth Press

Go to **www.newgrowthpress.com** or call **336.378.7775** to purchase individual minibooks or the entire collection. Durable acrylic display stands are also available to house the minibook collection.